Pages on the Floor

A Curated Poetry Collection

Janay Blakely

Pages on the Floor: A Curated Poetry Collection

By Janay Blakely

Published by J Blakely Holdings

Copyright © 2022 Janay Blakely

Cover by Janay Blakely

ISBN: 979-8-9856544-0-0

Print edition

Dedicated to Mom and Dad for never once letting me give up on the dream.

Table of Contents

On *Race*

Poplar Trees: *an homage to Abel Meeropol's poem "Strange Fruit"/ Billie Holiday's song "Strange Fruit"*

Ain't no more poplar trees

Their season having seemingly passed

Black bodies blowing in the breeze

Limbs gone limp like withering vines

Ain't no more poplar trees

But their sap still permeates the air

Drips onto the sidewalk

Creeps into the crops

Staining even the stars

Ain't no more poplar trees

Confederate leaves waving high in the sky

But their roots run deep

Tripping up the feet of those attempting in vain to pass by

No

Ain't no more poplar trees

Yet there's still strange fruit a plenty

picked before their time

My Grandfather's Hands

Brown sullied dirt molded into life

>These are my grandfather's hands

Large enough to swallow all of the night sky

Hailing from deep Mississippi, remnants of its great river run thick and strong as bulging veins

>These are my grandfather's hands

Hard and calloused, conditioned from years of pulling weeds, the pricking of thorns

From sunrise 'til sunset

>Burnt pages of parchment with illegible messages

>Cuban cigars, hand rolled and sickly sweet

>Cracked wood of antique tables

>Dusty air of the Deep South

>The darkness of a cotton field at midnight

>>Of an empty house

These are my grandfather's hands

Gemini

I once thought you and I were connected

Two sides of the same coin

Bound by the melanin that coats our DNA

A shared history

A shared pain

I thought

You and I

Were two sides of the same coin

Left spinning from the turn of someone else's hand

Forced to seek solace in one another

I thought a great many things

Yet it would seem I thought wrong

My back is covered in bruises

Markers of the places where your fist sought to connect
with my soul

My thick skin is nothing but scar tissue

Remnants of the words you spat at me

So, tell me dear brother

Why is it I that still comforts you

Sings you songs to act as a balm for your wounds

Decorate my chest with the arrows that were surely
aimed at you

Present to you, myself, on a silver platter

A living sacrifice

A pain that will never heal

A hurt that no one should ever know

Dear brother

Help me to discover

Why is it you who harms me so

No Monsters Under the Bed

How many kids do you want?

Optimistically as a child

     5, 7, 10

Now, none

Because he will be brown

The color of the soil from whence we came

Crosses upon which lambs were sent for slaughter

Freshly varnished mahogany coffins

At five he will come barring the scars of a playground
rendezvous with dragons and asphalt

After using the healing powers of hugs

After wiping away the sweat and grim of the day

He will ask, as he is tucked in,

     "Are there any monsters under the bed?"

And I will reply, head hung low

     "no"

They would never wait conveniently while you slumber

Green skin and boils as easy identifiers

Red eyes bright and menacing

Talons with which to peel back your skin

My darling,

 if only it were that simple.

No, they stand in wait

Ready to pounce in the middle of broad day

How can I reassure him he is safe?

Knowing

That as I measured him for a cradle, they measured him for a grave.
While other children get to raise their hands to answer questions in school, I am teaching him to announce "My hands are up, please don't shoot"

Tell him to believe the posters imploring him to be all he can be

When really, if we look at things statistically,

I am not raising a man

But rather a future chalk outline on the street

His blood used to paint that familiar red, white, and blue motif

Because I will name him

      Trayvon or

      Michael or

      Kendree

I will call him beloved

They will name him

      Thug or

      Criminal or

      Villain

And they will pronounce him dead

Because I do not have the energy to learn lullabies to soothe his soul when he is six

And then hymns to soothe mine when he is gone at sixteen

Staying up at night wondering when the world stopped seeing him as my baby

Trying to locate the exact moment the boys in blue stopped being my friends

I refuse to birth a prince and have his crown turned to a shackle

I refuse to produce kings only to have them kept as slaves

Backs used as baseboards to line alabaster floors

Like his great grandfather

> His grandfather and

> His father before he

I refuse to bury my son long before he has had the thought to bury me

Because this is something I will never understand

That the greatest monsters my child will ever face are nowhere near the underside of his bed.

Pick One

You can be colored

The sin of your lineage evident in the pigment of your skin

Hair coiled towards the heavens, seeking to uproot itself

Forced to learn the not so sacred art of the genuflect

You're allowed to have hips that sway to the rhythm of old and tattered Baptist hymns

Have a voice with the echoes of a grandmother's prayer begging for safekeeping

To wade in the water

To have hands that never ball into fists

You're free to be colored

You just can't be colored and

Can't be colored and have a lisp that pierces the air like a whistle

Can't be colored and sell cigarettes on the street

Can't be colored and buy candy and a drink

Can't be colored and play music loudly

Can't be colored on a couch fast asleep

Can't be colored and live the American dream

Can't be colored and have a picnic

Can't be colored and go for walk

    Or a jog

    Or a run

Can't be a colored child playing with a toy gun

Can't be colored and sit at the lunch counter

    Or drink from the water fountain

    Or swim in the pool

Can't be colored and pray to a God who may or may not hear you

Can't be colored and live this life with ease

You can be colored

You just can't be colored and breathe

Speaking in Tongues

There is no greater temptation than that of taming the tongue

Constricting its movements

Forcing it to wrap around perfect pronunciation

Familiarizing itself with only the King's English

Abandoning colloquial dialects

Putting firmly in the past words like ain't and sto'

Adopting instead firm e's and harsh r's

No lackadaisical dips and drawls inspired by Sunday dinners of black-eyed peas and neckbones

No more difficult task is there than that of balance

The donning of a chameleon's coat

Disappearing into an all-white sea

Walking the tightrope between colonizer and colonized

How I long to freefall

Embrace the guttural call of the old Negro spiritual

Envelop myself in languages lost to time and lashings

Devour every word uttered in a midnight prayer

Escape the shackles of pre-sanctioned sentences

I want to unleash the full power of my tongue

The Marvels of Ancestry

Some of us were kings and queens

Cloaked in purple and majesty

Crowned with the authority of deities

Some of us were paupers and thieves

Turned loose to the streets

Bellies begging for crumbs and filled with yearning

Yet we were people just the same

Brown

I want to forget the color brown

The color of coagulated blood staining the pure white stockings of little girls playing under church steeples

Of freshly turned unmarked graves

Of police canines

Of slave ships

I want to forget brown

The color of tar that stains everything it touches

Of hands that linger a little too long, holding me a little too tight

Of predators masquerading as kings

Of crosses that I must silently bear with grace and dignity

I want to forget brown

Soul sucking

Back breaking

Heart aching brown

I want to forget brown as if being blue would have made a difference

Dear Little Black Girl

Dear little black girl

The one with the name so majestic it confuses foreign tongues until its letters tumble out of mouths falling graciously to the floor

The one whose skin is set so deep you could plant a garden in it

The one whose hair bobbles sing the song of a thousand jungle gym warriors running off into battle

To the one whose hips swing to a rhythm not yet acquainted with the blues

To the one with the scar on her left knee

I see you

Can spot the North Star in your smile and follow it all the way to the freedom of your laughter

I hear you

Can recognize your cocoa butter smooth voice in the midst of a full Baptist choir

I feel you

Can trace your fingerprints in the palm of my own hand

I am you

Having grown and weathered storms you are not quite yet
ready for

Dear little black girl

When you feel discouraged say a small prayer for us both

May the destination never take precedence over the
journey

May love be the foundation upon which we build our
lives

May we never lose sight of what's inside

May our heads always be held high

May our enemies be laid low

May we remember our divinity wherever we go

In the name of all that makes us holy

Amen

On *Love*

Colors

I loved you

Boldly

On full display

In technicolor

Too bad your eyes only understood black and white

Such a shame you were colorblind

Mango Season

I will always love mango season

Succulent sweet slices

Over ripe fruit still begging to be eaten

Nectar dripping from eager lips like adolescent apologies
into the ears of the broken hearted

Infections start in those hollow cavities called chests

I once heard mangoes, antioxidants, were good for that

Two sets of feet run through the mangroves

Am I chasing you or are you chasing me?

I can't quite remember

Air thick with the smell of nature's perfume
Tree trunks become confessionals

Supposed true love having long since etched its initials
into the wood

We shared one last mango before you retreated to some
northern land

Even after all the years, I still don't know what to do with
the seed

I wonder if they have mangoes after their snow

I wonder when mango season will return

And if it will bring you, as it has always done, back to me, again

Drink Up

You complained that I am too hard to swallow

Opinions too big

Laughter too loud

Skin like alligator leather

Too tough

Too thick

And yet when I was quiet

And delicate

And quaint

Never once did you look my way

I couldn't be your cup of tea

But I am my own shot of whiskey

And I intend to drink up

Bodies

I thought being easy would be easy

Laying with new lovers every night whose tongues spoke
different languages than mine

We only understand

       Legs

              Hands

Bodies banging against each other

Boulders colliding at full force

I thought being easy would be easy

See, I know about hands

Hands claiming other body parts for land

Caressing thighs

Hands

       Pressing on ribs

       Silencing inhibitions

I know about hands like I know about bodies

Piling atop one another

      Their creases and folds

I thought being easy would be easy

Turns out being easy ain't easy at all

Because when bodies fling themselves at each other

Hearts have a tendency to pop out of chests

There lies mine

      Broken

      Battered

Tried to grab it up off the floor

Resettle myself

But you had already taken it

Placed her in the bottom of your shoe to be carried off to another body that was missing parts

Whose own heart had already ceased beating

New beds turned into coffins carelessly tossed into the ravine.

Burned alive on a pyre of bodies I thought I understood.

Laundry Day

Let us

You and I

Lay out our dirty laundry

Allow the sun to illuminate the corners we had hoped were forgotten

Show us the holes in our trust now threadbare

Scrub clean the stains emblazoned across our starched shirts

Scarlet letters announcing betrayal

Let us

You and I

Pull out our wash basin

Old and battered and rusted

Scrub away our secrets till the fabric is bright and new

Resole the shoes that once led us away from one another

Repair the pleats in our pants where promises were undone through the obligations of life

Let us

You and I

Fully launder our lives

Eden

Would you love a flower that bloomed in the dark?

Sit in awe as each petal unfurled defiantly

Stem swaying in a non-existent breeze

Leaves curled upward towards an onyx sky

Would you inhale the scent of my skin?

Help steady my roots planted in rocky and shallow
ground

Watch as my spirit germinates in the calm and quiet of
solitude

Transpose me to a garden and guard me fiercely

Would you help me grow?

Renewed

Every seven years all the cells in your body are replaced

> The knee you scrapped at five

> The cheek that caught all your tears at nineteen

> The spot between your inner thighs she
> discovered at twenty-three

Gone

On the nights my soul is splintering

When heaven does not seem so close

When the memory of your caress begins to fade into
obscurity

I remember

> Only seven years

Then I will have a body you have never touched

Butterflies in my chest having been released from their
cage

Stronger ribs now reinforced to control this ragged heart

Lips that have never known your distinct brand of
sweetness

A lifeline redrawn to go on without you

Seven years until your fingerprints are erased from my skin

But what of the indentations left on my heart

      The blood in my veins

      The essence of my soul

      My dreams which I once gave you to hold

Space

I used to never understand the concept of a vacuum

Not a Hoover sucking up secrets swept haphazardly under the rug

A vacuum in space where nothing exists

No air

No sound

No movement

Then you left and suddenly it clicked

A place in space devoid of any light

Of any feeling

Of any hope

Of any meaning

I now understand the physics of a heartbreak.

Not Another Love Poem

In all these years, I have never written a poem about you

Placed pen to parchment and allowed myself to fully bleed

To cleanse

To confess

To find the words to label the strange dance between you and I

Me creating rhythms

You, stumbling about on two left feet

Following along awkwardly

Could never write for you a love poem

For we were never lovers

Emotions innocent and pure

Eternally connected

We were strangers who both loved jazz

The smoothness of it all

Acquaintances who would fall into the same bed

The problem with the love poem

It is an antiquated thing

Reserved for those whose hearts still beat

Whose souls are in rapture

For hands already being held

For lovers

For others

For those who are not us

So, this is not a love poem

It is a eulogy for all that we were

A dedication to the things we could have been

A dissertation dissecting all that we weren't and couldn't
be

This is many things

But it is certainly not a love poem

A Letter to My Future Lover

I am writing in the hopes that you exist

That in a sea full of eight billion people

There is still a solitary island upon which I can find respite

A piece of land I can call my own

Dear future lover,

When we meet, I do not expect it to be love at first sight

For I have been blinded by beauty before

Lured by the shine and sparkle of promise

Of hope for something new

When I first see you,

I only pray it feels warm

Like a kiss from the sun

Dear future lover,

When you hold me

Do not be alarmed by the grooves in my skin

Markers where others tried to mold me into being their own

Stretch marks evidence of the places I expanded

Attempting to fill their emptiness

Decorated in fingerprints that don't belong to me

Dear future lover,

Please ignore this songbird's sad melodies

Low and rumbling

Like the thunder announcing a coming storm

Feathers that ruffle at a single touch

Having had to choose between flight and fight for far too long

Be gentle

I beg

With this battered soul

On *Life and Self Reflection*

Fierce

I am the guardian of my fate

I am the protector of my soul

Reflections

I once thought I met God

In the silent cacophony of an expanding universe

In that queer expanse between the sky and the rest of the cosmos

Sitting on the lonely island of solitude dangling on the bottom of the hooks of question marks

I met God

We sat and pondered

Or rather, I pondered, and He knew,

 The questions I had long harbored in the silent cavern of a quivering breast

Pouring out

Laying in a crescent moon counting stars

I want to say he answered

Patted my head and said

"There there my child. For I know the plans that I have for you. Plans that you should not fail, but prosper"

It is hard to know what is said when conversations traverse universes

Constantly repeating

      'Can you hear me now"

I thought I met God where the ocean hugs the sun

Cradling each other, matching yin and yang symbols, as one

I thought I met God right at the space where the sidewalk ends

Sitting in between the semicolons where life could have ended but really has only just began

Standing before the mirror

Deep within my eyes

I saw God, the Universe, and I all at the same time

One Day

One day, living won't seem like a punishment

A sentence handed down by a malevolent master

The weight of the world won't rest solely on your brittle shoulders

Bones threatening to break under the strain of it all.

Someday, your breath won't rattle your insides

Whistling as the gales sweep through the empty hollow between your ribs

Back shivering in your own frigidness

Eventually, there will be a break in the clouds

The sun warming the skin you'd forgotten

Your spine will unfurl, no longer stuck in the fetal position

Your eyes will see more than the shadows of your demons

One day, you will be well

One day, you will be whole

Long

This life is long

Like winding roads twisting through fields that stretch out for miles

Like the wisps of willow trees blowing knowingly in the wind

Like summer days and the feeling of being suffocated by sweltering heat

Like the staccato song of a caged bird with clipped wings

This life is long

Long as the lifelines of my grandmother's palms made smooth from years of kneading biscuit dough and weaving our family's histories through my hair

Long as Pentecostal skirts sweeping against the ground after service

Long as the flight of monarch butterflies

This life is long

Just about as long as the blink of an eye

I Am a Poet

I am a poet

Not because of my mastery of language

Or my proficiency in prose

Or even my ability to write no matter which way the wind blows

Not because of my recognition or titles to my name

Certainly not because of some fleeting sense of fame

Allow me to make this very plain

None of these things are how a poet is made

I am a poet because I am human

Because I laugh with my whole belly

Because I feel with my whole heart

Because I understand my fellow man even if our lives are worlds apart

I am a poet because I see the world

Every shade

Every hue

I am a poet
And so are you

Happy Poems Don't Win Pulitzer Prizes

When asked why I do not write happy poems I always have a simple reply

"I have never seen a happy poem win a Pulitzer Prize"

Audiences do not give standing ovations to tales of merriment

Literary critics scoff at the notion of amusement

There are no awards for tales of joy

As a poet

You are not permitted to be happy

For poet is just another word for a tortured soul

So, as it stands

I do not write happy poems

Selfishly

I keep my joy a secret

Lock it deep within my chest for the moments when neither the sun nor the moon can light my path

Collect smiles and peals of laugher

Hoard them as a dragon does its treasure

Guard them doggedly

    As the artist does their work

    As a mother does her baby

    As God does us all

I do not write happy poems

because some parts of the soul are too private to lay bare

Too personal to share

Fleeting

Delicate

Longing to be handled with care

Exhale

I have decided to release my demons

Those close companions only I know

To pluck the shrapnel of loneliness out of my skin

Piece by piece

I am choosing to let you go

Return you back to the depths from whence you came

Knowing even still that we may one day meet again

I am choosing to seek out the sun

To let it alight the holes now found in my patchwork of a soul

To pick up my needle and sew myself back together

On this day, the day of my rebirth

I am finally choosing to exhale

In Honor of Francis de Sales

Is there a patron saint for poets?

A protector of those who feel all things too deeply

Who looks after those armed only with similes and metaphors?

Who absolves us of the sin of being human?

On whose ears does a poet's prayer fall?

Rain

I love when it rains

The way the earth smells

Clean linen

Freshly bloomed flowers

Redemption

Awake

Today I have found myself awake

Having managed to escape an all-consuming dark
slumber

Stretched out my limbs and found them all to be perfectly
intact

Today

My shadow didn't resemble a ghoul, but rather, a long-
lost friend

My mind declared a cease fire

Its constant attack finally relenting

And today my voice held a song I had not heard in many
a moon

Today

On this day

I have hope anew

Memories

Sometimes I revisit my old poems

Pick the grains of salt from past tears off the pages

Sprinkle them over myself

Preserving my soul

In the hopes we both survive the winter

On *Family*

Jacob's Ladder

I always watch cartoons with my nieces and nephews
because when I was little my father did the same with me

He was the closest thing I knew to a giant

To God

I shed a tear whenever I hear old hymns

Their curious blend of hope, strength, and sorrow remind
me of my grandmother's voice

How its vibrato sinks into your bones, so it's felt long
after she is done singing

On Saturdays I wander into cigar shops and inhale the
scent of my grandfather

Earthy

Familiar

I carry peppermints because my mother had them tucked
away in her pocket book every Sunday morning

My aunt adorns herself in silver each day, so I wear a
single bracelet to give myself some shimmer

I repeat the prayers of my other aunt because her
whispers go directly from her lips to God's ears

I hear my sister's voice every time I laugh

I see my brothers' faces every time I look in the mirror
and smile

I am a patchwork of my lineage

Walking evidence of my family tree

I am them

They are me

Acknowledgements

Usually, acknowledgements can be quite lengthy as many people are involved in the traditional writing process. That being said, the writing of this book has been anything but traditional. This labor of love has been brought together by a small team of dedicated likeminded individuals who only wanted to see me live out my dream, and for that, I must give thanks.

I would first and foremost like to thank my parents Rickey and Tammy Blakely. Thank you for seeing my love of reading as a child and fostering it. Thank you for the countless nights of reading and rereading my poetry, for talking me off the ledge every time I thought I wasn't good enough, and for never letting me let the dream die. Without you, not only would this book not be possible, I also wouldn't know what it means to go out fearlessly into the world as my most true and authentic self. Thank you, a thousand times over.

Next, I would like to thank my beta readers and editors Mrs. Amy Scott and Mrs. Christina Kerr. Thank you for recognizing my potential in high school and always demanding more of me. You both helped me to push my creative limits and mold me into the writer that I am today. Your edits helped to build a better poetry collection and your reassurance helped me to stop doubting myself and my ability. I am forever grateful that you both were placed in my life and were willing to help me with my life's dream. Thank you.

Finally, I would like to thank my dear friend Loren. You have been there for me during some of my darkest hours that inspired several of the pieces in this collection. Thank you for your constant support, for being a sounding board, a graphic designer, a consultant, and so much more. Thank you for believing in me. Thank you for not letting me let this project fall to the wayside as so many have before. To quote the Golden Girls "Thank you for being a friend".

Without you all I would still be writing my poetry in my journal without ever sharing it with the world.

Thank you for helping me pick my pages off the floor.

Author Interview

1. When did you first discover you wanted to be a writer?

I know that it is cliché to say that this is what I have wanted to do my entire life, but it is the truest answer to this question. I have wanted to be a writer since I discovered that there were people who had the privilege of writing professionally. Even when I began to look into positions in the corporate world that seemed to be a good fit for me, some form of writing or story telling was always involved. It is what my heart's passion is.

2. Is being a poet hard?

Anybody can be a poet. All you need is the desire to be one and have something to say. You do not have to rhyme, or have a thousand stanzas, or even have a deep profound message. All you need is the desire to write and then to do so. So, in that regard, no; being a poet is not hard at all. What makes it hard is the desire to excel in your craft. I think that goes for any craft really. If you are not satisfied with mediocrity then you have to study, constantly evolve, and elevate your skill level.

3. What was the most difficult part of writing 'Pages on the Floor'?

Editing was, by far, the most difficult part of the process. I had help from three people when it came down to editing and proofreading. It is difficult because you are allowing someone else to see your work which requires a special sort of bravery by itself. Then, you are giving them the sole job of finding everything that is wrong with your work. When they find grammatical and spelling errors you wonder how you weren't smart enough to find those yourself the first time around. When they have suggestions as to pieces that should be cut from the book or stanzas that should be changed, it feels not like they are rejecting pieces of the book but rather pieces of my soul. My writing is very personal to me, so any changes people suggest I often take to heart.

I am, however, learning to better accept edits/suggestions. I even enjoyed the last round of editing because it allowed me to show my growth as a writer.

4. What recommendations do you have for anyone looking to write their own book?

My advice, which I believe you will find to be the advice of any kind author, would be to simply write the book! For years I read other people's work and thought to myself 'I can do better than that'. Then I proceeded to sit on my laurels and do nothing. The only difference between myself and an aspiring author is that they have not published their book yet. Write the book, the poem, the song. Whatever it is that lingers in your mind day in, and day out is what you are meant to be doing. Now, as far as advice beyond that I would say do your research on the publishing process. Writers, we are an enthusiastic bunch when it comes to our writings. Once it is written you may want to charge headfirst into a publishing office and show them your book. That is not how the process works. Look into whether you want to publish traditionally or self-publish. Do you need an agent? Who are your contemporaries in your genre? Who is your writing for? Things can become very granular very quickly.

So, first we write the book. Then, we consider how and when we would like to get it out into the world.

About the Author

Janay Blakely was born and raised in sunshine filled Miami, Florida. While much of Janay's work is far from comical, she is a self-proclaimed comedy aficionado, spending much of her time (pre-and post-pandemic) binging comedy specials on Netflix.

For inquiries please email: jblakelyholdings@gmail.com